Coloring book for adults and kids amazing sharks image for design

This coloring book
is belongs to

____

____

____

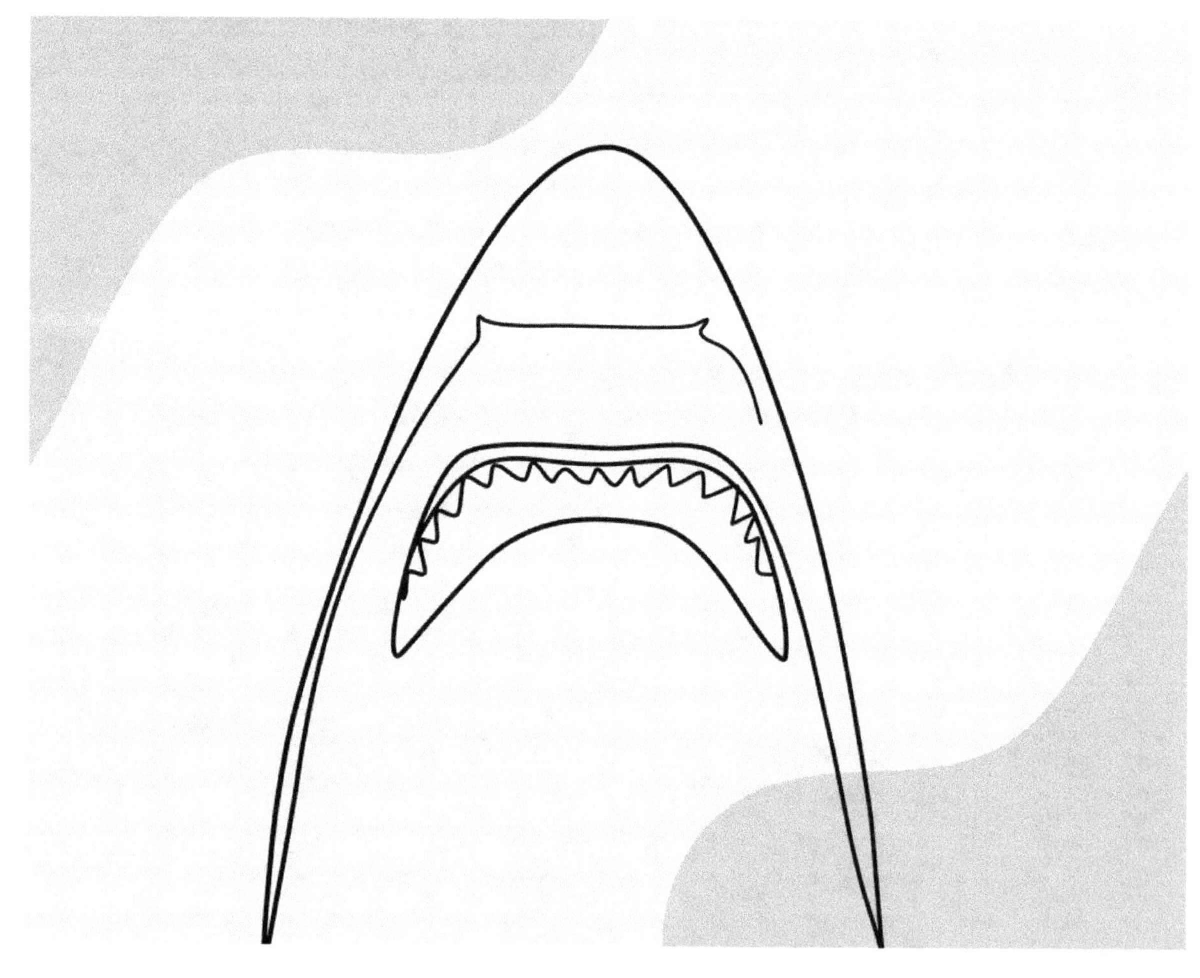

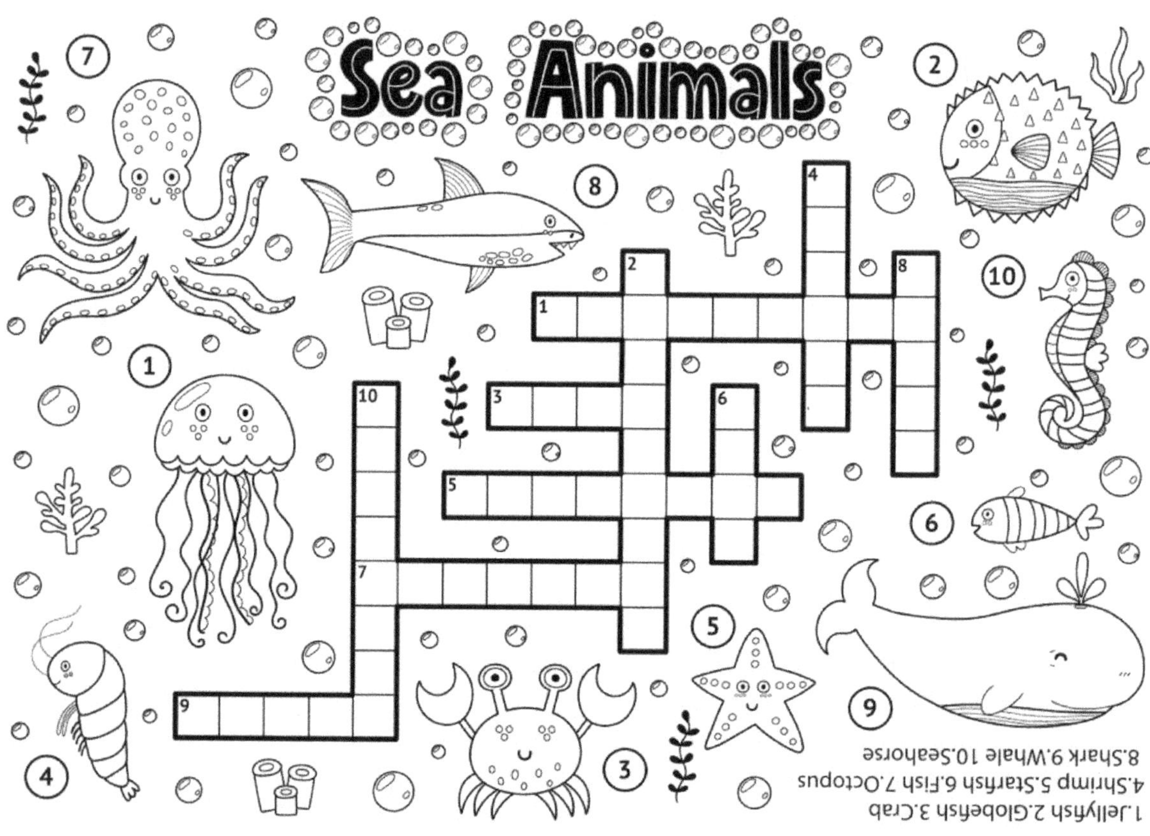

Sea Animals
1.Jellyfish 2.Globefish 3.Crab
4.Shrimp 5.Starfish 6.Fish 7.Octopus
8.Shark 9.Whale 10.Seahorse

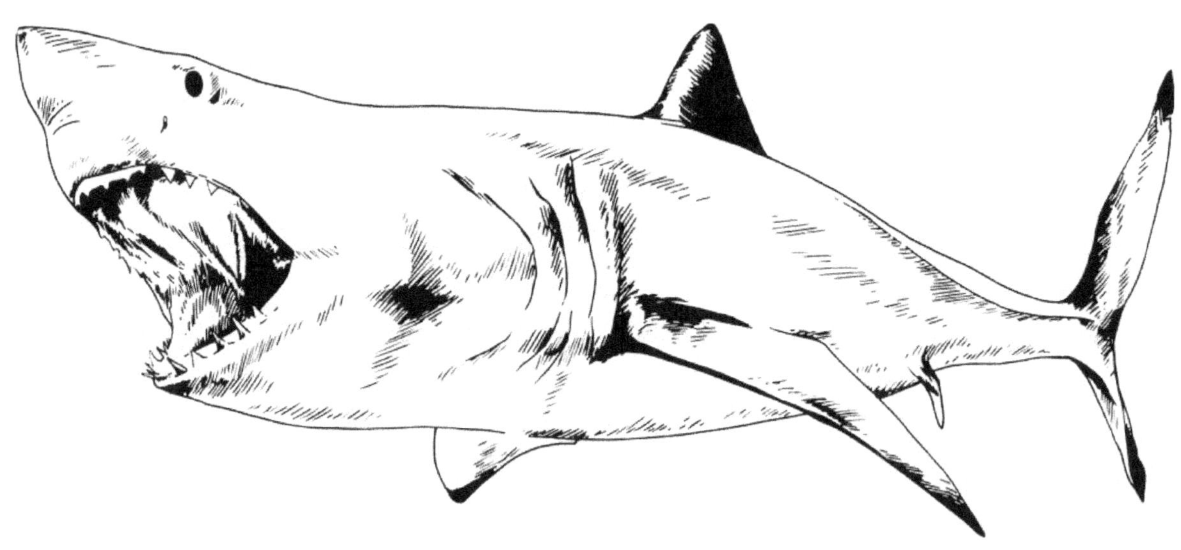

Make a wave

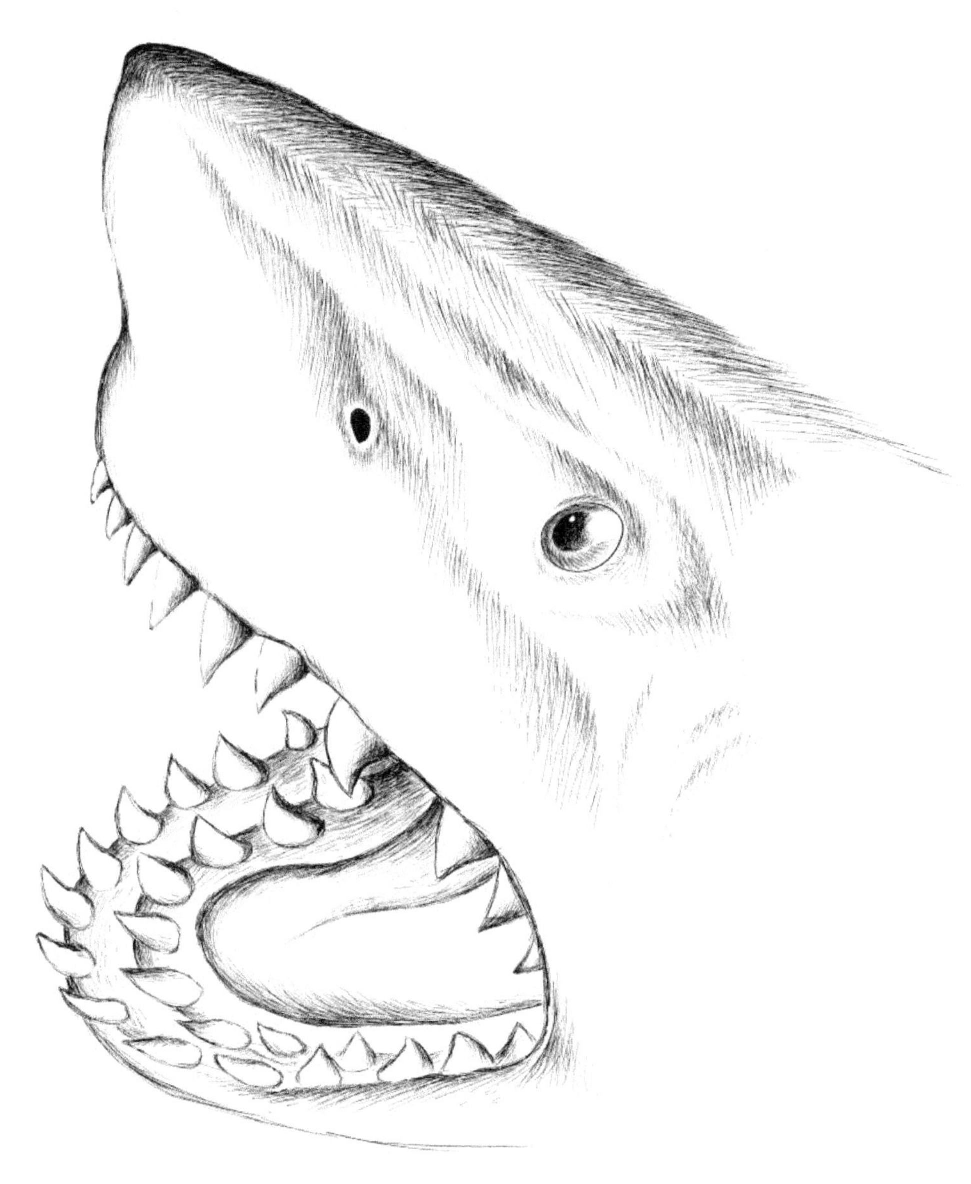

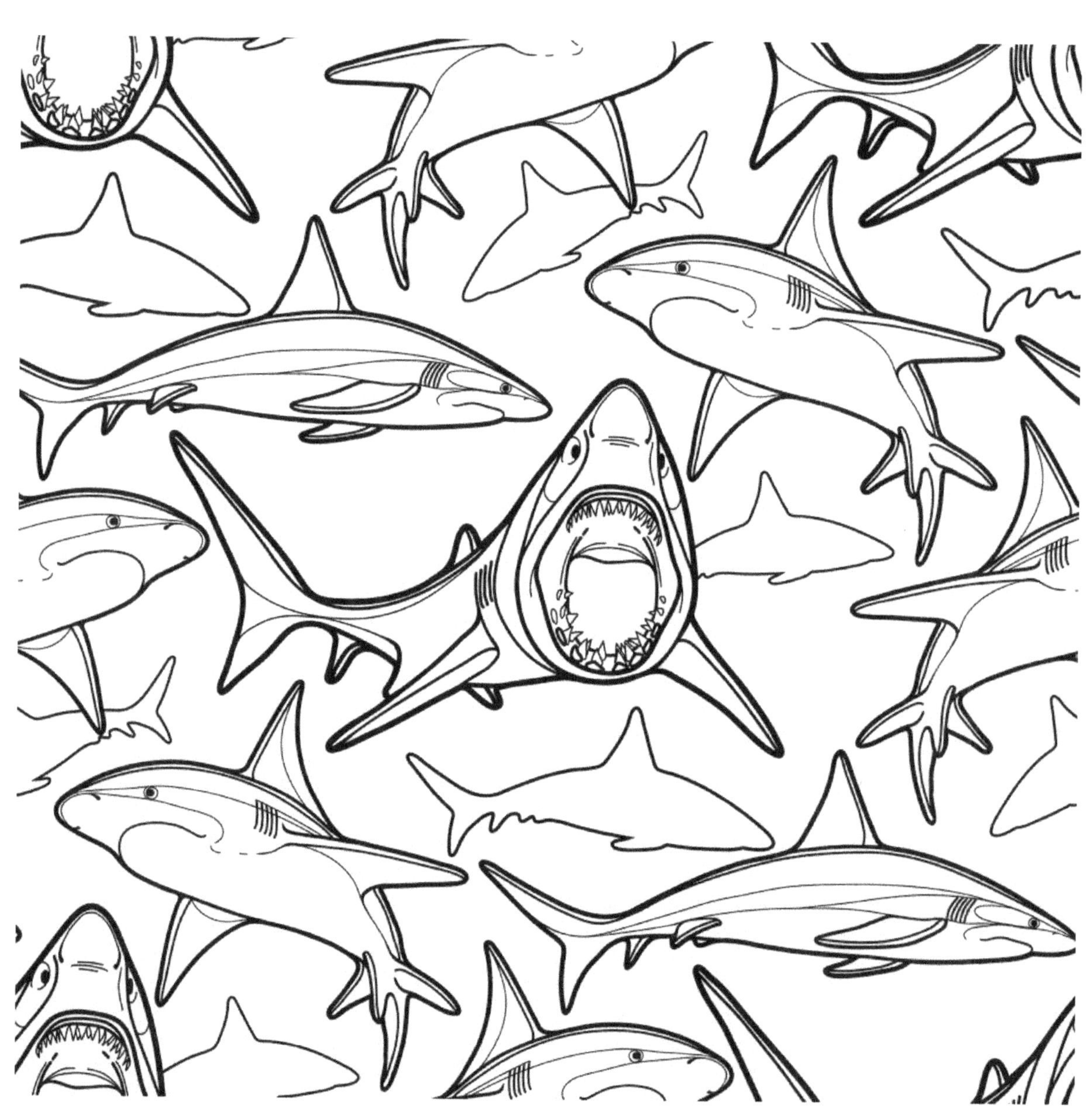

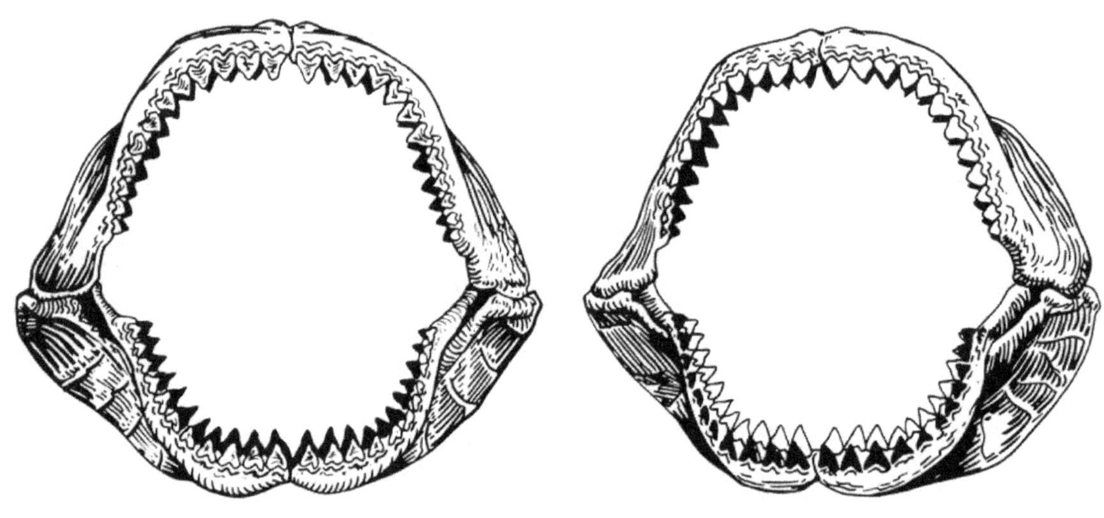